W9-BLL-560

Nations of the Plains

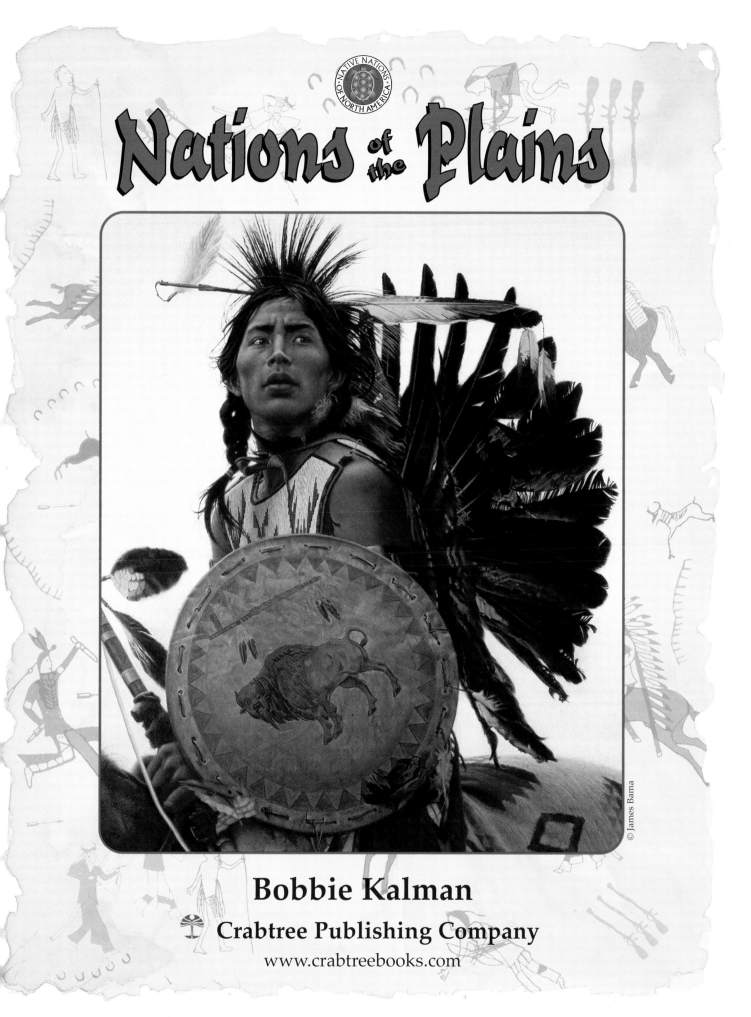

© James Bama

Bobbie Kalman

🌲 **Crabtree Publishing Company**

www.crabtreebooks.com

Nations of the Plains

Created by Bobbie Kalman

(Dedicated by Deanna Brady)
For Kala, Gwynne, and Grandpa

Author and Editor-in-Chief
Bobbie Kalman

Research
Deanna Brady
Kate Calder

Editor
Deanna Brady

Copy editors
Heather Fitzpatrick
Kathryn Smithyman

Computer and Graphic design
Kymberley McKee Murphy

Production coordinator
Heather Fitzpatrick

Consultant
Deanna Brady, Corporate Board Director,
   PHO2000 American Indian Outreach Programs;
   American Indian Changing Spirits
Professor J.S. Milloy, The Frost Centre for Canadian
   and Native Studies, Trent University

Photographs and reproductions
Marc Crabtree, 30 (bottom)
The Greenwich Workshop, Inc. Shelton, CT: James Bama, *Young Plains Indian*
   (detail), 1; *The Vision Place* (detail), 18; *Sioux Subchief* (detail), 21;
   Tom Lovell: *Listening for the Drums* (detail), 9; *Fire in the Buffalo Grass* (detail), 13;
   Time of Coldmaker (detail), 16; *Four Times to the Sun* (detail) 20;
   Blackfeet Wall (detail), 25; *Walking Coyote and the Buffalo Orphans* (detail), 28;
   Howard Terpning: *The Signal* (detail), 9; *Old Country Buffet: The Feast* (detail), 12;
   The Staff Carrier (detail), 14; *Offerings to the Sun* (detail), 18; *Paints* (detail) 19 (top);
   Stones that Speak (detail), 19 (bottom); *Scout's Report* (detail), 22;
   Chased by the Devil (detail), 23; *Telling of the Legends* (detail), 24; *Medicine Man
   of the Cheyenne* (detail), 27; *Hope Springs Eternal-The Ghost Dance* (detail), 29;
   Blackfeet Storyteller (detail), back cover
The Kansas State Historical Society, Topeka, Kansas: Jakob Gogolin,
   Railroad (detail), page 27 (bottom)
© permission of Lazare & Parker, page 8 (top left)
Alfredo Rodriguez, *Legends of the Past*, page 31
Charles M. Russell, *Indian Women Moving* (detail) 1961.47, oil on canvas, 1898,
   Amon Carter Museum, Fort Worth, Texas, cover, page 14 (top)
Charles M. Russell, *Three Generations* (detail), courtesy of The R.W. Norton Art
Gallery, Shreveport, LA, page 6
Smithsonian American Art Museum, Washington, DC/Art Resource, NY: George
   Catlin, *Mandan Village-A Distant View*, page 10
Smithsonian Institution Photographic Services, Washington, DC,
   page 30 (top and middle)

Illustrations
Barbara Bedell: 7 (bottom), 10 (bottom), 15 (bottom), 16, 17 (top), 19, 21 (bottom), 22
Margaret Amy Reiach: hide backgrounds, 7 (middle), 8 (right), 12, 17 (bottom),
   18, 20, 21 (top), 23 (left)
Bonna Rouse: 4, 7 (top), 23 (right)

Crabtree Publishing Company

www.crabtreebooks.com   1-800-387-7650

PMB16A	612 Welland Ave.	73 Lime Walk
350 Fifth Ave.	St. Catharines	Headington
Suite 3308	Ontario	Oxford
New York, NY	Canada	OX3 7AD
10118	L2M 5V6	United Kingdom

Cataloging in Publication Data
Kalman, Bobbie
   Nations of the Plains / Bobbie Kalman.
      p. cm. -- (Native nations of North America)
   Includes index.
      ISBN 0-7787-0368-1 (RLB) -- ISBN 0-7787-0460-2 (pbk.)
   This book introduces children to the customs, languages, and
traditional ways of life of several Native nations that lived on
the Great Plains of North America.
   1. Indians of North America--Great Plains--Juvenile literature. [1. Indians
of North America--Great Plains.] I. Title. II. Series.
E78.G73 K37 2001
978' .00497—dc21
                                          LC2001017296
                                          CIP

CONTENTS

THE GREAT PLAINS

The Great Plains is a vast region that stretches nearly one million square miles. This flat area was formed millions of years ago during the Ice Age by the slow movement of enormous **glaciers**. On its eastern outskirts are forests and rivers, rolling hills, and valleys. The central section is wide and flat, with few trees or lakes. Before the 1800s, miles of grass covered this huge open space. The eastern areas had long grasses and were called the **Prairies**. The Central Plains had short grasses.

Plains Cree

Assiniboine   *Métis*

Blackfeet

NORTHERN PLAINS

Crow   *Hidatsa*
Mandan
Arikara

CENTRAL PLAINS

Northern Cheyenne

Sioux

Northern Arapaho
Pawnee

Southern Arapaho

SOUTHERN PLAINS

Southern Cheyenne   *Osage*
Kiowa   *Quapaw*

Plains Apache

Wichita

Comanche

*The **homelands** of the Plains nations changed as European settlers came west. This map shows where some nations lived before the 1800s.*

grasslands

mountains

 mixed forest

 evergreen forest

desert

 scrub

The Great Plains stretches from Indiana and Illinois in the East to the base of the Rocky Mountains in the West. It extends north into Alberta, Saskatchewan, and Manitoba and south to Oklahoma, Texas, and Mexico.

The Great Plains

A difficult place to live

The open areas of the Great Plains presented many survival challenges. The climate varied from hot, dry weather in the summer to freezing temperatures in the winter. There were few edible plants, and water was hard to find. The people who lived out on the open plains relied on the **bison**, or buffalo, as their source of food, clothing, shelter, and tools.

The people of the Plains

For thousands of years, dozens of groups of **indigenous**, or Native, people lived on or near the Great Plains. Many shared the same hunting and farming methods, but they were not one single large **nation**, or cultural group. They differed in the styles of dress they wore, the languages they spoke, and the customs and traditions they practiced. Each **tribe**, or nation, was unique, and each had its own **homeland**.

FAMILIES, BANDS, NATIONS

The people who lived in a Plains camp belonged to certain nations, but they also belonged to smaller groups. Each nation was composed of several **bands**, or groups of families who lived together in their own villages or camps. Within many Native nations, individuals also belonged to **clans**. Each clan was made up of people who shared a common **ancestor**. Some Nations had many clans, and others only a few or none. When people visited other bands, they stayed with clan relatives, just as you might stay with relatives in another town.

Community support

Life on the Plains was difficult, but Native people helped one another survive. Members of bands, clans, and families always supported one another. If a person or family was suffering or did not have enough food, others in their band or clan gave these people the things they needed. Native people were taught to put the needs of the community before their own desires. They measured their prosperity by the gifts they gave to others, rather than by the possessions they kept for themselves.

*Many Plains families lived in tents called **tipis**, which belonged to the women of the camp. This picture shows three generations of a family: a son, his parents, and his grandfather. The mother and father belong to different clans.*

PLAINS HOMES

The people of the Plains lived in homes that suited their environment and lifestyle. Some lived in permanent homes and others in portable homes, which they set up in temporary camps.

Tipis

A tipi is a large cone-shaped tent made of long poles tied together at the top and covered with buffalo hides. The top is left open so that smoke from the fire can escape. The doorway of the tipi often faces east, where the sun rises. The base-poles are set in the other three directions.

painted tipi

Grass and hide houses

People who lived on the Southern Plains sometimes built grass-covered homes. To construct one, they laid thick thatches of grass over a framework of long poles. Other such homes were covered with hides instead of grasses.

thatched hut

Earth lodges

People who lived in permanent villages often built large homes called **earth lodges**. These lodges were made of wood and covered with **sod**, or grassy earth. The builders created a round wooden framework on which they laid willow branches, dried grass, and sod. Eventually, grass grew over the sod, so each lodge blended into its surroundings and looked like a small hill. Inside, the floor was dug a foot below the surface of the ground, forming a ledge on which to sit. Food was stored in storage containers dug into the soil. A long, narrow entrance kept out the wind, and a hole at the top released smoke from the fireplace.

earth lodges

PLAINS COMMUNICATION

Plains sign language became the basis for the modern sign language that is used today by people who have hearing difficulties. The man above is making the sign for "tipi."

Dozens of different languages were spoken on the Plains. Most of these belonged to six main **language groups**: Siouan, Caddoan, Algonkian, Athabaskan, Kiowa-Tanoan, and Uto-Aztecan. Still, even languages that were related were unique in many ways. With so many languages, people from different nations sometimes had difficulty understanding one another.

sign for "buffalo"

Sign language

Sign language allowed Plains nations to communicate. People made **signs**, or motions with their hands and arms, which represented words and messages. There were hundreds of signs. Many Native people could speak easily and gracefully with their hands. Sign language enabled nations to trade with one another, make peace agreements, and warn others of danger. It also helped Native people communicate with Europeans who had learned some of the hand signs.

sign for "gone"

History in pictures

Until the 1800s, Plains people did not have alphabets or written languages. They often recorded events by drawing pictures. For each year that passed, they drew a picture on a buffalo hide. These "history hides" were called **winter counts** because many people counted the years of their lives by the number of winters that had passed. For every "winter," there was a picture showing an important event that had happened sometime during that year.

Long-distance communication

People of the Plains used many kinds of non-verbal signals to communicate with others from a distance. In the picture above, two men listen to a drum signal from their camp. Smoke signals were often used, as well. They were made by holding a blanket over a fire and then lifting it to release thick puffs of smoke, which could be seen miles away. Timing the intervals between puffs of smoke created different messages. Scouts also learned how to screech like hawks or howl like wolves to give a warning or a location without making their presence known to enemies. Other warning signals included pictures drawn on trees and flashes of sunlight reflected off shiny objects such as mirrors or pieces of glass.

By waving a hide in the air, this **scout** *is sending a signal that buffalo are nearby.*

9

LIFE BEFORE THE HORSE

Before modern horses were brought to North America from Europe, most Native people had to stay on the forested outskirts of the Plains, close to rivers. They built permanent villages and were **sedentary**, living mainly in one place, although they went on short trips to hunt buffalo and other wild animals. During the summer, they grew crops such as corn, beans, pumpkins, sunflowers, melons, and squash. They also gathered wild berries, seeds, nuts, roots, and greens. While the weather was warm, they dried and stored as much food as they could so they would have enough to eat during the long, cold winters.

Going short distances

People were able to travel only short distances because they had to walk wherever they went. They did not accumulate many possessions because they had only dogs to transport them. A dog could not carry or pull more than a small tipi with a few fur blankets and, perhaps, a child. The tipi poles were attached to a dog's harness to make a carrier that the French called a *travois*. In winter, the dogs pulled sleighs.

Some Native nations, such as the Mandan and Hidatsa, lived in permanent villages such as the earth-lodge village above.

A difficult life

Water was too heavy to carry very far, so people had to live near water sources. Most Plains people hunted buffalo that roamed near their villages. When the buffalo stayed away, people had to travel out onto the open plains to hunt them. Finding enough food to eat was often a challenge! Very few nations lived on the vast, open, grassy areas where there was little rainfall and the land was unsuitable for growing crops.

Nomadic nations

People who lived year-round on the open plains relied on the buffalo for their entire livelihood. These **nomadic** people knew where the buffalo roamed each season and followed them to their different grazing areas. Nomadic nations lived in tipis and traded buffalo meat and **hides**, or skins, for crops grown by farming nations. Other nations were **semi-nomadic**. They lived in permanent villages but also went on hunting trips.

DEPENDING ON THE BUFFALO

Native people were always grateful for the food and materials that the buffalo provided. They tried not to waste any part of the animal. Its meat was eaten fresh, dried to make **jerky**, smoked, or made into ground **pemmican** patties. The skin was **tanned**, or preserved as leather, from which clothing, tipi covers, moccasins, blankets, and pouches were made. Bones were carved into tools, utensils, and beads. Hooves were boiled for glue, and **sinew** was used for thread and bow strings. Every part of the buffalo was useful. Even the intestines and tongue were eaten, and the stomach was used as a cooking pot.

The buffalo jump

Before the Plains nations had horses, hunting buffalo on foot with handmade spears and arrows was difficult, time-consuming, and dangerous. A trick known as the **buffalo jump** greatly increased the success of a hunt. The hunters created a V-shaped pathway with large stones, which led towards a cliff. They then shot burning arrows into the grass around the pathway. The grass fires frightened the animals onto the narrowing path. Sometimes the hunters wore wolf skins over their head and shoulders, frightening the buffalo into a stampede. The panicked buffalo then ran at full gallop over the cliff, landing in a corral area below.

(left) Grass fires frightened the buffalo, making them run over a cliff.
(below) Chasing buffalo or herding them into a buffalo jump was much easier on horseback!

HORSES ON THE PLAINS

© Howard Terpning

Thousands of years ago, there were small horses in North America, but they disappeared long ago. When Spanish explorers brought European horses with them to North America in the 1600s, the Native people they met had never seen a horse. Some of the horses escaped from the Spanish settlements and ran off to live on the plains. They had babies, and their herds grew in size. Eventually, horses were readily available to Plains hunters, who caught them, traded them, and learned how to tame and ride them.

The horses obtained by Plains hunters were smaller than the modern horses bred today. When Native people saw them for the first time, they called them "big dogs," "mysterious dogs," "sacred dogs," or "sky dogs." Why do you think they chose these names?

14

Valuable horses

Horses were valued greatly. The more horses a person had, the more fortunate and successful he or she was considered to be. A person who had many horses was thought to be prosperous indeed! Before asking a woman to marry him, a man tried to acquire as many horses as he could. Horses were traded, given as gifts, and stolen from other nations.

Bringing a new way of life

Horses changed the way of life of the Plains nations. On horseback, people were able to hunt buffalo more easily and worry less about feeding their families and bands. People could move faster than the buffalo and follow the herds quickly as the seasons changed. With horses to move their homes and supplies, entire bands could relocate easily and set up large seasonal camps. Pushed westward by the growing European settlements of the eastern prairies, some of the nations who had lived in permanent villages became nomadic hunters on the open plains.

*Since hunting was less difficult on horseback, men had more time to devote to warfare. They formed **warrior societies**, raided enemy camps, and engaged in an activity called "counting coups. " **Coup** is a French word for "hit." Hitting an enemy with a stick or stealing his horses counted as a coup.*

Older horses were often used as pack animals. With the help of horses, families could carry bigger tipis and more supplies with them as they traveled over the plains. Horses could also carry people long distances.

15

NORTHERN PLAINS NATIONS

© Tom Lovell

By the 1800s, more than thirty Native nations lived on the Plains. The Northern Plains included land that is now Montana, North Dakota, Alberta, Saskatchewan, and Manitoba.

Its northeastern areas had hills, forests, lakes, and rivers, but the rest was mostly flat, open prairie. The short summers of this region were mild enough to grow vegetables, but winters were bitterly cold and stormy, and deep snow covered the ground.

Arikara

Mandan, Hidatsa, Arikara

The Mandan and Hidatsa were Siouan speakers who grew crops of corn, beans, and squash and went on hunting trips for buffalo. They were later joined by the Caddoan-speaking Arikara. These nations lived in earth-lodge villages, shown above. Such villages were important trading centers for nomadic tribes who wanted to trade buffalo hides for crops. They also provided a link between the European fur traders and Native buffalo hunters.

Mandan

Assiniboine

The Assiniboine were nomadic Siouan-speaking people who lived in Saskatchewan and traded furs with the European settlers. They were known as the Stoney because of their method of cooking with hot stones. They formed an **alliance** with the Plains Cree nation.

Plains Cree

The Algonkian-speaking Plains Cree tribe was one of the larger tribes in the early 1800s. There were more than 15,000 Plains Cree scattered across a large area of the Northern Plains. In fact, the Cree occupied the largest area in North America! They lived on the prairies of Saskatchewan and Alberta. The Plains Cree and Assiniboine both became dependent on hunting buffalo and other animals. They sold furs and hides to European traders.

The *Métis*

Over time, more and more European settlers began new lives in North America. In Canada, many French-men married Native women. Their children were of both European and Native heritage.

People with this mixed heritage became known as *Métis*. *Métis* is a French term meaning "mixed" backgrounds. The *Métis* hunted buffalo on the Plains and participated in the fur trade. They lived mostly in the area that is now southern Manitoba.

This Assiniboine warrior is wearing a loose-fitting hide shirt. Over his shoulder is a buffalo robe with the fur side worn against his body. He holds a protective shield.

*The Mandan, Hidatsa, and Arikara used **bullboats** to travel on rivers. Bullboats were made of two buffalo hides stretched over a frame made from willow branches.*

17

The Blackfeet

The Blackfeet comprised one of the most powerful **confederacies** in the Northern Plains. It had more than 15,000 members and was made up of three closely related nations: the Siksika, the Blood, and the Piegan. The Blackfeet are Algonkian speakers. They lived in areas that are now Saskatchewan and Montana. After they acquired horses, they moved farther west to the edge of the Rocky Mountains. Among neighboring nations, the Blackfeet were known as fierce warriors. They accepted challenges and fought bravely. The Blackfeet lived in nomadic camps and hunted buffalo throughout the year. They also harvested wild rice in the fall. They wore beautiful outfits decorated with **quillwork** and fringes, and their tipis were colorfully painted.

The Blackfeet felt close to the spirits that guided their lives and often went into the woods to leave offerings, which they tied to the trees, as their ancestors had always done.

The Crow

The Crow are a Siouan-speaking tribe that was once part of the Hidatsa nation. They were sedentary farmers who lived in earth lodges and raised crops along the Missouri River. They **migrated** westward and became truly nomadic buffalo hunters on the Northern Plains. The Crow used dyed porcupine quills and beads to adorn their ceremonial dress and greased their bangs to stand straight up. The Crow preferred to ride **"paint"** horses, shown above, which were bred to look as though they had been painted.

The Crow were great trackers. They looked for signs, such as this turned-over stone, to tell if someone had recently traveled in a certain area.

19

CENTRAL PLAINS NATIONS

The Central Plains is a large area that spreads over what is now South Dakota, Nebraska, Kansas, Iowa, and Missouri. Most of this area is open plains, but some of it is covered in hilly, forested terrain.

The Pawnee

The Pawnee tribe lived in permanent earth-lodge villages. They were farmers who also went on trips during the summers to hunt buffalo and other game such as deer and otter. The 10,000 Pawnee were the largest Caddoan-speaking nation in the area.

The Cheyenne

The Cheyenne are Algonkian-speakers who were originally village dwellers and farmers. They are believed to have originated north of the Great Lakes. They became nomadic buffalo hunters. Their original tribe separated into two branches. One branch stayed in Wyoming and became known as the Northern Cheyenne. The other branch moved south into Kansas and became the Southern Cheyenne. The Northern Cheyenne allied themselves with the Sioux, and the southern group, with the Kiowa and Comanche.

© Tom Lovell

Warriors relied on their shields to protect them in battle. They constructed them to be sturdy and decorated them with drawings, furs, and feathers. Before battle, this Cheyenne warrior raises his shield four times to the sun and then brushes it against the grass four times to bring into it the protection of the sky and Earth. Four is considered a sacred number.

The great "Sioux" nation

The name "Sioux" is a French variation of an Algonkian word. The people who came to be known as the "Sioux" originated in the woodlands of the upper Mississippi and were part of a large confederacy. Their tribal names described their seven Council Fires.

As they moved west onto the prairies, the seven divisions developed three variations of their language in different regions. Spreading from east to west in their territories, these dialects are now called Dakota, Nakota, and Lakota. All three words mean "allies" and are sometimes used to refer to three segments of the greater Sioux Nation.

The "Sioux" were originally farmers who also hunted, but the western Lakota speakers, the Teton, later became nomadic buffalo hunters.

Arapaho

The Arapaho are an Algonkian-speaking tribe. Their nation was made up of about 3,000 people. It was a nomadic group of buffalo hunters who had similarities with the Cheyenne and Teton Sioux. The Arapaho adorned their clothing with bone, paint, and quills, just as their neighboring nations did.

Today, people often think of the Plains cultures when they think of Native North American people. Tipis, buffalo robes, headdresses, and buffalo-hunting are all images of Plains life that have been made popular by movies. This Dakota (Sioux) warrior wears a large feather **bonnet** and bear-claw necklace and carries a lance and shield.

© James Bama

21

THE SOUTHERN PLAINS

The Southern Plains includes land that is now Texas, Oklahoma, Arkansas, and Northern Mexico. This area has a warmer climate because it is farther south than the other areas of the Great Plains. The tribes who lived here did not have to worry about building homes that kept out extreme cold, wind, and snow.

Comanche

The Comanche were the most skilled horsemen of the Southern Plains. They lived in tipi camps and hunted buffalo. Comanche bands were independent of one another. They spoke a version of the Shoshone language. Other Shoshone speakers, such as the Ute and Western Shoshone lived west of the Plains.

*The **scouts** who rode ahead of war parties were known as "wolves" because they often wore wolf skins. They believed they could borrow the wolf's skills.*

Osage

The Osage people speak a Siouan language. They were farmers who lived in permanent villages in what is now Missouri. The Osage also hunted buffalo. They often decorated their clothing and blankets with pictures of horses and hands.

Quapaw

The Quapaw people lived in **palisaded** villages in an area that is now Arkansas. Their homes were dome-shaped lodges that were covered with bark, hides, or grass. Within their villages, important buildings were built on mounds, where council meetings and **ceremonies** were held. The Quapaw made beautiful pottery.

Wichita

The Wichita tribe lived in the area that is now Oklahoma. It was the largest Caddoan-speaking group in the south. These agricultural people lived in dome-shaped grass houses. **Wichita** means "raccoon-eyed." It describes this nation's practice of face-painting and tattooing.

Kiowa and Plains Apache

The Kiowa nation speaks a language that is related to that of the **Pueblo** nations of the Southwest, with whom they traded. The nomadic Kiowa and Plains Apache lived on the Plains long before most other nations moved there. They allied themselves with the Comanche.

These Apache riders try hard to stay ahead of a hot-weather whirlwind of dust and debris on the southern Plains.

© Howard Terpning

BELONGING TO THE LAND

© Howard Terpning

The Native people who made the Plains their home knew how to make the most of what the landscape had to offer. They paid very close attention to their surroundings. They carefully noted the sound and the smell of the wind so they could anticipate approaching storms or dry weather. They relied on running streams and springs for fresh water. They knew which berries and roots were safe to eat and which herbs could be used to help heal injuries and illness. They showed their gratitude for the sun, winds, and rain. They respected the Earth. Although Native people felt attached to their home-lands, they did not feel that they owned the land. They felt that they belonged to the land and were its children, whose job was to maintain it for future generations. Their role was to respect the plants and animals and make sure the environment was protected.

OWNING THE LAND

The Europeans who came to North America had a very different idea about land. They thought of land as a valuable possession. They wanted to own and change it. They felt that they had "discovered" this continent, even though millions of people already lived here. They claimed the land for their countries. Native people found the idea of land ownership difficult to understand. They signed **treaties**, or agreements, with the Europeans, thinking they were merely granting them equal use of the land.

Get off my property!

The people who **settled**, or came to live on, the homelands of the Native nations assumed that they then owned the land. They wanted the Native people to stay off their "property." They also treated the animals that were on the land as their property. When Native people tried to hunt on their old homelands, they were shot or put in prison for trespassing. As more Europeans came to the West, more land was taken from the Native people.

These Blackfeet warriors form a "wall," determined to defend their homeland against the European invaders.

© Tom Lovell

CHANGES ON THE PLAINS

After the Europeans arrived, changes came quickly to the Plains. They came in the form of soldiers, traders, farmers, prospectors, diseases, guns, and alcohol.

The fur traders

The furs or hides of animals such as beaver, deer, antelope, and buffalo were very valuable to Europeans, who sold them to people in Europe and eastern North America. The Native people, who were excellent hunters, traded the furs for food, tools, cloth, beads, and guns.

Lewis and Clark

After the United States "bought" the Great Plains from the French as part of the Louisiana Purchase, the American government was worried that French and British traders would continue to control the fur trade in the West. It sent out explorers Lewis and Clark to **survey** the western lands and bring back reports about the plants and animals and about the Native nations that lived there.

More fur trade and settlers

The Lewis and Clark expeditions made the fur trade grow even bigger! More and more Native nations began relying on the fur trade for their livelihood. The Lewis and Clark expeditions also encouraged settlers to move to the West. People packed their possessions in wagons and made the long trip across the Plains, hoping to own large areas of land and begin new lives. Soon, thousands of wagon "trains" dotted the flat landscape.

Diseases, alcohol, and guns

As Europeans moved west, they brought new diseases, which spread quickly. Native people had never been exposed to the bacteria that caused such diseases. Their bodies had no resistance to the germs, and many became sick and died. Some bands and villages were completely wiped out by the diseases, and others were left much smaller in number. Another novelty brought by the Europeans was alcohol. Native people had never drunk alcohol, so even a little affected them badly. Alcohol made them ill, sometimes causing death. Guns also caused many deaths among the nations.

Even the strongest Cheyenne medicine could not deal with the germs of the Europeans!

The gold rushes

In the mid 1800s, gold was found in California and several other areas. Word spread quickly to the East. Thousands of **prospectors** and their families traveled west as fast as they could, passing through the Native homelands. Native people were seen as a threat, so soldiers were sent west to protect the prospectors.

Thousands of prospectors came in search of gold.

Railroads bring more settlers

After the gold rushes, railroads were built across both Canada and the United States. Trains brought thousands more settlers to the Plains, where the government gave them Native lands to farm. By this time, there were not many buffalo left, but passengers on trains were nevertheless encouraged to shoot buffalo from the windows. Taking away the food supply of the Native people would make them even more dependent on the government!

As railroads were built and buffalo herds were wiped out, Native people protested by ripping up rail ties.

END OF A WAY OF LIFE

© Tom Lovell

Several factors led to the deaths of the huge herds of buffalo that once roamed the Plains. European horses and cattle ate the grasses the buffalo needed as food, and settlers fenced their new land so the buffalo could not graze on it. They killed buffalo for only their hide or tongue and left the carcasses to rot on the plains. Native hunters also killed thousands of buffalo to trade the hides for European goods. By the early 1900s, the great herds had disappeared from **overhunting**. The food source of the Native nations was gone, and people were starving on the Plains!

Starving Native nations were forced to sign treaties agreeing to live on isolated lands set aside for them, called **reservations** in the United States and **reserves** in Canada. Many of these lands were unsuitable for farming. In return for living on reservations, people were supposed to receive food and other supplies such as materials and tools. The government did not provide enough food, however, and much of the food that was sent was stolen or arrived spoiled.

This couple is helping some starving buffalo orphans so these calves will grow and have babies of their own.

Life on the reservations

Americans and Canadians wanted the people of the Plains to give up their nomadic way of life and support themselves as the settlers did. The land on the reservations was divided into small areas, which were allotted to individual families. Families were given meager housing and were expected to farm the land, but it was often of such poor quality that nothing would grow on it.

Little hope

The reservations were overcrowded and unsanitary, causing diseases to spread. There was little paid work and no hope for making life better. Native people depended on what little food and materials were provided by the government, and many became very depressed. The Ghost Dance, shown below, symbolized the last hope of the Plains people to bring back the buffalo and regain the old way of life.

© Howard Terpning

In 1889, a Paiute medicine man named Wavoka had a dream that his people, who had been killed by soldiers, were living happily in the afterworld. This dream led to the Ghost Dance, which spread like a new religion. People hoped that by dancing, they might bring back their relatives. Soon, nations across the Plains were dancing to bring back their old way of life. This idea angered the government. Near a place called Wounded Knee, soldiers tracked down and massacred more than three hundred starving women, children, and elderly Native people.

NEW WAYS, OLD WAYS

These two photographs show the outward changes to children at the boarding schools. Children were made to feel ashamed of their Native cultures.

This boy is competing in a "fancy-dance" contest at a powwow. He has worked hard to perfect his steps.

In an attempt to change the way of life of future generations of Native people, the governments of both Canada and the United States removed Native children from their homes and sent them hundreds of miles away from their families to live in large boarding schools. At these schools, children were not allowed to practice their traditions and were forced to speak English, become Christians, and dress like Americans or Canadians.

Practicing their culture in secret

Although most Native people were prevented from conducting their ceremonies, speaking their languages, or wearing their traditional clothing, many tried to preserve their cultures in secret. Still, it was hard for these aspects of Native life to survive, since the people no longer had control over their lands or lives.

A new spirit

In the second half of the 20th century, Native Americans and Canadians began to revive their cultures, languages, and traditions. Many nations are now teaching their original languages to the children, and several have established tribal schools, colleges, and universities on their reservations. Tribes are striving to strengthen their rights as **sovereign nations**, which have control over their own people's lives and laws. Native people are also reclaiming their rich heritage through cultural activities such as music, art, dance, theater, and social gatherings called **powwows**.

INDEX

Legends of the past are also being revived in books and, again, through stories told by Elders.

GLOSSARY

alliance An association of two or more groups for the purpose of a common goal

ancestor Someone from whom someone else is descended, especially before grandparents

band A group of Native people who live together in a camp or village

bison A family of large, shaggy animals, often called buffalo

bonnet A headdress decorated with items such as feathers, beads, and porcupine quills

buffalo jump A method of hunting in which hunters cause buffalo to stampede over a cliff

ceremony A formal act or ritual performed following customs or a set of actions

clan A group of people who are related by a common ancestor

confederacy An alliance of groups or nations

counting coups Keeping record of the "hits" or humiliations inflicted upon an enemy

glacier A large body of slowly moving ice

hide The skin of a dead animal, which is treated and used to make clothing, tipi covers, and other useful items

homeland The area in which a nation lives

indigenous Describing people or things that are native to, or born in, a specific area

jerky Meat that has been dried so it can be stored and eaten without cooking

language group Several languages that are similar to one another because they share roots in a single language

migrate To move to another place

nation A large group of people who share origins, customs, laws, leaders, and language; a tribe

nomadic Describing people who live in temporary camps and travel often, following herds of animals that they hunt

overhunting Hunting too many animals and causing them to become endangered or extinct

paint (horse) Describing a horse bred to have large patches of white color; a pinto

palisaded Describing an area surrounded by a tall fence made of wooden poles with sharp points

pemmican A food made of dried buffalo meat that has been pounded into paste, mixed with fruit, and shaped into cakes

plain A grassy area of land

Plains Referring to the Great Plains

powwow A Native gathering and ceremony that includes music and dancing

prairie A vast area with long grasses

Prairies Grass-covered areas of the Great Plains in the United States and Canada

prospector A person who searches for gold or other valuable natural resources

quillwork Crafts using feather or porcupine quills

Pueblo Describing people who lived in large dwellings made of adobe, called pueblos

reservation (reserve) A specific area of land set aside for Native people

scout A person who is sent ahead to explore or spy in order to obtain information about landscape or the location of animals or enemies

scrub An area with shrubs and short trees

sedentary Describing a group of people who settle permanently in one area

semi-nomadic Describing people who live in permanent homes part of the year but travel during other seasons to gather plants or hunt

settler A person who moves to a new place and makes it his or her home

sinew A tissue that connects muscle to bone

sovereign nation A self-governing group that is not ruled by another nation

survey To make a detailed map of an area

tanning A process of making leather from the hides of animals by soaking them in a solution and drying and stretching them

treaty An official written agreement between two groups that settles disputes over such issues as land ownership and hunting rights

tribe A group of families, clans, or bands that shares common ancestry, culture, and leaders

warrior society A club whose members mediate fights, patrol areas, help others who need assistance, and take part in acts of war

 1 2 3 4 5 6 7 8 9 0 Printed in the U.S.A. 0 9 8 7 6 5 4 3 2 1